Scan Me to Connect

Copyright

About the Author

Pablo Puig is a cloud computing expert, consultant, and author specializing in helping international businesses navigate the complexities of China's cloud ecosystem. With years of experience working with AWS China, Alibaba Cloud, Tencent Cloud, and Azure China, Pablo has provided strategic guidance to enterprises, startups, and IT professionals looking to expand their cloud operations in one of the world's most regulated and rapidly evolving markets.

Pablo's journey into China's cloud computing landscape began when he encountered firsthand the challenges faced by foreign companies in establishing and maintaining cloud environments within China. From navigating ICP licenses, compliance frameworks, and cross-border data transfer restrictions to optimizing network performance under the Great Firewall, he has worked extensively with global and local cloud providers to design solutions that align with Chinese regulatory requirements while ensuring operational efficiency.

Beyond his consulting work, Pablo is a thought leader and educator passionate about demystifying China's cloud infrastructure for a global audience. He has authored several books, including "AWS China: From Zero to Hero. The Complete Guide" and "Azure China: The Complete Guide" which have become essential resources for IT professionals, cloud architects, and enterprises looking to deploy and manage cloud solutions in China. His books provide practical insights, real-world strategies, and step-by-step guidance to overcome the unique challenges of operating cloud environments in China.

Pablo has also been a speaker at industry conferences and corporate training events, sharing insights on digital transformation, data security, and cloud architecture in China.

His expertise in cross-border cloud strategy, compliance frameworks, and AI-driven cloud solutions has helped numerous companies scale their operations successfully in the Chinese market.

Through this book, Pablo aims to equip IT professionals, cloud architects, and business leaders with the knowledge and tools needed to navigate the complexities of cloud computing in China. Whether you're an enterprise looking to expand into China, a cloud professional seeking deeper insights into Chinese regulations, or simply curious about the future of cloud technology in China, this book serves as a comprehensive guide to overcoming challenges and unlocking opportunities in one of the most unique cloud markets in the world.

Table Of Contents

CHAPTER 1
OVERVIEW OF THE CHINESE CLOUD MARKET

Lesson 1
Understanding the Chinese Cloud Market

T he Chinese cloud market has rapidly evolved over the past decade, becoming one of the largest and most dynamic cloud ecosystems globally. With a combination of robust government support, a surge in digital transformation across industries, and a burgeoning middle class demanding more digital services, China's cloud computing landscape presents both unique opportunities and challenges. Major players such as Alibaba Cloud, Tencent Cloud, and Huawei Cloud dominate the market, offering a wide range of services that cater to different segments, from small startups to large enterprises. Understanding the nuances of this market is essential for IT professionals and business leaders looking to tap into its potential.

Government policy plays a crucial role in shaping the Chinese cloud market. The Chinese government has prioritized digital infrastructure development as part of its broader economic strategy, encouraging investment in cloud technology through various initiatives and funding programs. The "New Infrastructure" initiative, for example, emphasizes the importance of cloud computing, big data, and artificial intelligence in driving economic growth. Additionally, regulatory frameworks around data security and privacy are evolving, which necessitates that cloud professionals stay informed about compliance requirements and how they impact service delivery.

The competitive landscape in China's cloud market is characterized by rapid innovation and aggressive pricing strategies. Domestic companies often leverage their local knowledge and expertise to develop services tailored to the specific needs of Chinese businesses. For instance, many cloud providers offer localized solutions that address regional preferences and regulatory requirements. This environment compels IT professionals to continually update their skill sets and knowledge base to remain relevant. Understanding the strengths and weaknesses of various providers, as well as their service offerings, is essential for making informed decisions about cloud adoption. Adoption trends in the Chinese cloud market reveal a growing preference for hybrid and multi-cloud strategies among enterprises.

Businesses are increasingly recognizing the need for flexibility and scalability in their cloud deployments, often combining public and private cloud solutions to meet their operational needs. This shift is driven by the desire to optimize costs and enhance data security while ensuring compliance with local regulations. As cloud professionals navigate this landscape, they must develop strategies that align with these emerging trends, ensuring that their organizations can take full advantage of the benefits offered by various cloud models.

Finally, the future of the Chinese cloud market holds immense potential as advancements in technology continue to reshape the industry. Innovations such as edge computing, artificial intelligence, and machine learning are set to redefine how cloud services are delivered and consumed. For business leaders and IT professionals, staying abreast of these trends and understanding their implications will be critical for strategic planning. By embracing the opportunities presented by the evolving cloud landscape, organizations can position themselves for success in an increasingly digital economy.

Lesson 2

Market Size and Growth of the Chinese Cloud Computing Industry

China's cloud computing industry has experienced explosive growth, fueled by government-backed digital transformation, artificial intelligence (AI) investments, and rapid enterprise cloud adoption. As of 2023, the market reached RMB 616.5 billion (US$85.5 billion), reflecting a 35.5% year-over-year (YoY) growth. Projections suggest that by 2027, the market could exceed RMB 2.1 trillion (US$293 billion), effectively tripling in size within just four years.

Below is an overview of the industry's evolution and forecasted growth:

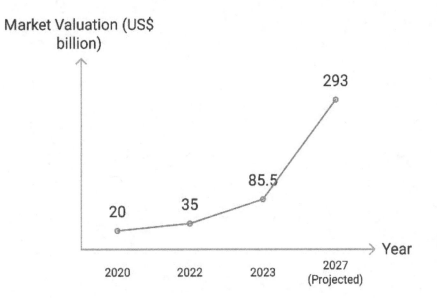

Growth of China's Cloud Computing Market
(2020-2027)

- 2020: The Chinese cloud market was valued at US$20 billion, primarily driven by e-commerce, gaming, and fintech adoption.
- 2022: The market expanded to US$35 billion, with post-pandemic digital transformation accelerating cloud investments across multiple sectors.
- 2023: The industry saw a 35.5% YoY increase, reaching US$85.5 billion, driven by AI-driven cloud solutions, government cloud initiatives, and the expansion of hybrid cloud architectures.
- 2027 (Projected): The total cloud computing market in China is forecasted to exceed US$293 billion, marking a threefold increase within just four years.

The Chinese cloud market is predominantly led by domestic providers, with the top three companies accounting for a significant portion of the market share:

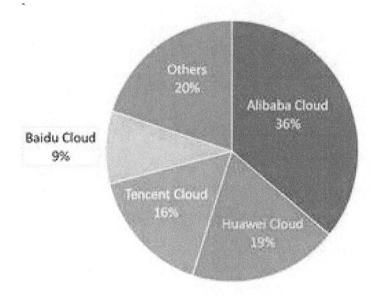

1. Alibaba Cloud: Maintains a leading position with a 36% market share as of the third quarter of 2024.
2. Huawei Cloud: Holds the second position with a 19% market share.
3. Tencent Cloud: Ranks third with a 16% market share.
4. Baidu: Ranks forth with a 9% market share.
5. Other providers (AWS China, Azure China, and local players): 20% market share.

Looking ahead, China's public cloud market is expected to more than double in size, growing from USD 32 billion in 2021 to USD 90 billion by 2025. This anticipated growth underscores the increasing reliance on cloud services across various sectors, including finance, healthcare, retail, and manufacturing.

The government's strategic initiatives, such as the "Internet Plus" and "Made in China 2025" programs, aim to integrate cloud computing with traditional industries, further accelerating market expansion. Additionally, advancements in technologies like Artificial Intelligence (AI), Internet of Things (IoT), and big data analytics are expected to drive further adoption of cloud services.

Lesson 3
Opportunities and Challenges in the Chinese Cloud Market

The Chinese cloud market presents a myriad of opportunities for IT professionals, business leaders, and cloud specialists. With the rapid digital transformation driven by government policies such as the "Internet Plus" initiative and the "Made in China 2025" strategy, there is a significant push toward cloud adoption across various sectors. Enterprises in industries ranging from manufacturing to finance are increasingly migrating to cloud solutions to enhance their operational efficiency and scalability. This trend is bolstered by the rising demand for big data analytics, artificial intelligence, and Internet of Things (IoT) technologies, all of which thrive in cloud environments. As a result, cloud service providers can capitalize on a growing ecosystem that values innovation and digital solutions.

However, the Chinese cloud market is not without its challenges. Regulatory hurdles remain a significant concern for both foreign and domestic players. The Chinese government imposes stringent regulations on data privacy and cybersecurity, which can complicate cloud operations and compliance. For instance, the Cybersecurity Law and the Data Security Law require companies to adhere to strict data localization requirements, limiting where data can be stored and processed. IT professionals must navigate these regulations carefully to avoid penalties and ensure that their cloud solutions are compliant. This necessity for compliance can create barriers to entry, particularly for international firms unfamiliar with the local legal landscape.

Competition in the Chinese cloud market is fierce, with major players like Alibaba Cloud, Tencent Cloud, and Huawei Cloud dominating the landscape. These companies have invested heavily in infrastructure and technology, resulting in a rapid evolution of their service offerings. For IT professionals and startups, this competitive environment presents both a challenge and an opportunity. While it may be difficult to gain market share against established providers, there is also room for niche solutions that cater to specific industry needs or offer innovative features.

Startups can leverage this by focusing on unique propositions, such as enhanced security features or specialized cloud applications, to carve out their place in the market.

Moreover, the increasing emphasis on sustainability and green technology is shaping the future of cloud computing in China. As environmental concerns gain traction, companies are being urged to adopt eco-friendly practices, including energy-efficient data centers and sustainable cloud solutions. This shift presents an opportunity for cloud providers who can offer environmentally conscious services. IT professionals should consider how their strategies align with these sustainability goals, as organizations are likely to prefer cloud partners who demonstrate a commitment to reducing their carbon footprint.

In conclusion, the Chinese cloud market offers a complex landscape filled with both opportunities and challenges. For IT professionals and business leaders, understanding the regulatory environment, recognizing competitive dynamics, and embracing sustainability will be crucial for success. The potential for growth is significant, but it requires a nuanced approach that balances innovation with compliance and sustainability. As cloud computing continues to evolve in China, those who can navigate these waters effectively will be well-positioned to thrive in this dynamic marketplace.

Lesson 4
Key Drivers of Cloud Adoption in China

The rapid adoption of cloud computing in China can be attributed to several key drivers that resonate with the unique economic and technological landscape of the country. One of the primary factors is the government's proactive stance on digital transformation and innovation. Initiatives such as the "Internet Plus" strategy and the "Made in China 2025" plan underscore the importance of integrating advanced technologies into traditional industries. These government policies not only provide a framework for cloud adoption but also offer financial incentives and support for businesses transitioning to cloud-based infrastructures, thereby accelerating the shift towards digital solutions.

Another significant driver is the increasing demand for flexibility and scalability among Chinese enterprises. As businesses strive to remain competitive in a rapidly changing market, the ability to quickly scale operations and adapt to consumer demands becomes crucial. Cloud computing offers a solution that allows organizations to expand their resources on-demand without the burden of heavy investments in physical infrastructure. This flexibility is particularly appealing to startups and small to medium-sized enterprises (SMEs), enabling them to leverage cloud technologies to innovate and grow without facing prohibitive costs.

Moreover, the rise of big data analytics is propelling cloud adoption in China. With the explosion of data generated by various sectors, organizations are seeking robust solutions to store, process, and analyze this information efficiently. Cloud platforms provide the necessary tools and infrastructure for big data analytics, allowing businesses to gain insights that drive decision-making and enhance customer experiences. The integration of artificial intelligence and machine learning capabilities within cloud services further empowers organizations to harness data in transformative ways, solidifying the cloud as an essential component of their strategic frameworks.

The competitive landscape of the technology sector in China also plays a pivotal role in cloud adoption. Major players such as Alibaba Cloud, Tencent Cloud, and Huawei Cloud are continuously innovating and expanding their offerings to capture market share.

This intense competition encourages the development of advanced cloud solutions, making them more accessible and affordable for businesses of all sizes. Furthermore, the emergence of specialized cloud services tailored to specific industries, such as finance, healthcare, and manufacturing, facilitates targeted adoption and integration, driving overall cloud penetration across the economy.

Lastly, the increasing focus on cybersecurity and data protection is influencing cloud adoption trends in China. As businesses move their operations to the cloud, concerns regarding data security and compliance with regulations become paramount. Leading cloud service providers are investing heavily in security measures and compliance frameworks to address these concerns, thereby instilling confidence in potential users. This shift towards more secure cloud environments not only reassures enterprises about the safety of their sensitive information but also aligns with the broader regulatory landscape aimed at enhancing data protection across the country.

Lesson 5
Managing Cloud Operations in China

Managing cloud operations in China requires a nuanced understanding of the unique regulatory landscape, technological infrastructure, and cultural considerations that influence the cloud computing sector. As the Chinese government maintains stringent oversight over data management and cybersecurity, IT and cloud professionals must navigate a complex framework of laws and regulations. This includes the Cybersecurity Law, which mandates that data localization is essential for any organization operating within its borders. Consequently, organizations must ensure that their cloud operations are compliant with local legislation while maintaining security and efficiency in their services.

Infrastructure plays a pivotal role in cloud operations in China. The country has made significant investments in its digital infrastructure, with numerous data centers strategically located across various regions. These facilities often provide advanced capabilities, including high-speed connectivity and access to cutting-edge technologies such as artificial intelligence and big data analytics. For businesses considering cloud deployment, understanding the geographical distribution of these resources can aid in optimizing performance and ensuring redundancy. Additionally, leveraging local cloud service providers can enhance service delivery and compliance with Chinese regulations.

Cultural factors also influence how cloud operations are managed in China. The approach to business relationships tends to differ from Western norms, with a greater emphasis on building trust and long-term partnerships. IT professionals must adjust their communication styles and engagement strategies to align with local expectations. This might involve more face-to-face interactions and a focus on relationship-building practices that resonate within the Chinese business context. Recognizing these cultural nuances can facilitate smoother collaboration with local stakeholders, thus enhancing the effectiveness of cloud operations.

Furthermore, as the demand for cloud services continues to grow in China, organizations must be agile and responsive to market trends. This involves not only adopting the latest technological advancements but also being attuned to the evolving needs of customers.

The rise of digital transformation initiatives across various sectors has increased the appetite for cloud solutions that offer flexibility and scalability. Cloud professionals should prioritize innovation and continuously explore new service models, such as serverless computing and multi-cloud strategies, to meet the diverse needs of businesses in China.

Lastly, effective management of cloud operations in China necessitates a strong focus on security and risk management. Given the complexities of operating in a highly regulated environment, organizations must implement robust security frameworks to safeguard sensitive data. This includes adopting best practices for data encryption, access control, and incident response. Regular audits and compliance checks should be integral to the operational strategy, ensuring that organizations remain aligned with both internal policies and external regulatory demands. By prioritizing security and compliance, cloud operations can thrive in China, fostering trust among clients and contributing to the overall growth of the cloud computing ecosystem.

CHAPTER 2
COMPLIANCE AND REGULATORY FRAMEWORKS IN CHINA

Lesson 1
Overview of Chinese Cybersecurity Laws

The landscape of cybersecurity laws in China is shaped by a combination of national security concerns, economic interests, and social stability. The Chinese government has implemented a series of regulations aimed at safeguarding its digital infrastructure and ensuring the protection of citizens' data. These laws reflect a broader strategy to control the flow of information, bolster national security, and foster the development of a robust domestic technology sector. Understanding this legal framework is essential for IT and cloud professionals operating in China, as it directly impacts compliance requirements and operational strategies.

One of the cornerstone pieces of legislation is the Cybersecurity Law, enacted in 2017. This law establishes a comprehensive framework for the protection of networks and the personal data of users. It mandates that network operators implement measures to safeguard data, conduct regular security assessments, and report incidents to authorities. Furthermore, the law emphasizes the importance of critical information infrastructure, requiring operators in key sectors to adhere to stricter security protocols. For businesses and cloud service providers, compliance with these regulations is not only a legal obligation but also a way to build trust with customers and partners.

In addition to the Cybersecurity Law, the Data Security Law (DSL) and the Personal Information Protection Law (PIPL), both introduced in 2021, further refine the regulatory landscape. The Data Security Law (DSL) categorizes data based on its significance to national security and the economy, imposing varying levels of protection requirements. This law emphasizes the need for data localization, particularly for data deemed critical or sensitive. Meanwhile, the Personal Information Protection Law (PIPL) mirrors international standards like the GDPR, setting forth strict guidelines on how personal data should be collected, processed, and stored. For cloud professionals, navigating these laws requires a thorough understanding of their implications for data handling practices and cross-border data transfers.

The regulatory environment is continually evolving, with the Chinese government frequently updating policies to address emerging cybersecurity threats and technological advancements. The emphasis on self-reliance in technology further complicates compliance, as domestic firms are often favored in government contracts and partnerships. For international companies looking to operate in China, staying abreast of these changes is crucial. Engaging local legal expertise and developing robust compliance strategies can mitigate risks associated with non-compliance, which can result in hefty fines and reputational damage.

Finally, it is essential for IT and cloud professionals to recognize the broader geopolitical context influencing China's cybersecurity laws. The tensions between China and other nations, particularly regarding technology and cybersecurity, have led to increased scrutiny and regulation of foreign companies operating within its borders. This climate not only affects operational decisions but also shapes the competitive landscape in the cloud computing sector. By understanding the intricacies of Chinese cybersecurity laws, professionals can better navigate these challenges, leveraging compliance as a strategic advantage in a rapidly changing environment.

Lesson 2
Data Residency and Sovereignty Requirements

Data residency and sovereignty requirements are pivotal considerations for organizations operating in China's cloud computing landscape. The country's regulatory framework mandates that data generated within its borders must be stored and processed locally. This requirement stems from concerns over national security, privacy, and the protection of sensitive information. As organizations increasingly migrate their operations to the cloud, understanding these regulations is crucial for compliance and risk management. Non-compliance can lead to significant penalties and operational disruptions, making it essential for IT and cloud professionals to stay informed about the evolving legal landscape.

The Chinese government has implemented a series of laws and regulations that govern data residency and sovereignty. The Cybersecurity Law (CSL), effective since June 2017, establishes the principle that critical data must be stored within China. This law is complemented by other regulations, such as the Data Security Law (DSL) and the Personal Information Protection Law (PIPL), which provide further guidelines on data handling and protection. Organizations must not only comply with these regulations but also ensure that their cloud service providers adhere to the same standards. This creates a complex environment where businesses must conduct thorough due diligence when selecting cloud partners.

Organizations must also navigate the requirements surrounding cross-border data transfer. China's regulations impose strict conditions under which data may be sent outside the country. These conditions often require organizations to conduct security assessments and receive government approval before transferring data abroad. Such measures aim to safeguard national interests and maintain control over data that could be deemed sensitive or critical. IT and cloud professionals need to establish clear protocols for data transfer and ensure that their operations align with the regulatory requirements to minimize risks associated with data breaches or unauthorized transfers. In addition to regulatory compliance, organizations must consider the potential operational impacts of data residency and sovereignty requirements.

Storing data within China often necessitates the adoption of localized cloud services that may differ significantly from global offerings. This can affect the scalability, performance, and availability of cloud solutions. Businesses need to assess their specific needs and determine the most suitable cloud architecture that aligns with both their operational goals and compliance obligations. Engaging with local cloud providers can also offer advantages in terms of understanding local market nuances and navigating regulatory challenges effectively.

Ultimately, data residency and sovereignty requirements present both challenges and opportunities for organizations in China's cloud computing ecosystem. By proactively addressing these requirements, IT professionals and business leaders can not only ensure compliance but also leverage local cloud capabilities to drive innovation and growth. A strategic approach to data residency can enhance data security, foster trust among customers, and support sustainable business practices. As the cloud landscape continues to evolve, organizations that prioritize compliance and adaptability will be better positioned to thrive in this dynamic environment.

Lesson 3
Compliance with Industry Standards

Compliance with industry standards in cloud computing is crucial for organizations operating in China, where regulatory frameworks are rapidly evolving. The Chinese government has implemented several laws and policies aimed at promoting cybersecurity and data protection. IT professionals must familiarize themselves with these regulations, such as the Cybersecurity Law (CSL), which mandates stringent requirements for data localization, network security, and incident response. Compliance with these standards not only ensures legal adherence but also builds trust with customers and partners who are increasingly concerned about data privacy and security.

In addition to national regulations, various international standards also play a significant role in shaping compliance strategies for cloud service providers in China. Standards such as ISO/IEC 27001, which focuses on information security management, and the General Data Protection Regulation (GDPR) from the European Union may influence operational protocols. Organizations seeking to expand their cloud services in China must align their practices with these standards to attract international clients and maintain a competitive edge. This alignment often necessitates investing in training and resources to ensure that employees are equipped to handle compliance requirements effectively.

The challenge of compliance is compounded by the dynamic nature of technology and the cloud computing landscape. Emerging technologies such as artificial intelligence and machine learning are being integrated into cloud services, which can complicate compliance efforts. IT professionals must stay abreast of both technological advancements and regulatory changes to ensure that their cloud systems adhere to industry standards. Continuous monitoring and auditing of cloud environments are essential practices that can help organizations identify compliance gaps and mitigate risks in real-time. Collaboration with industry associations and regulatory bodies can further enhance compliance efforts. Engaging with organizations such as the China Academy of Information and Communications Technology (CAICT) can provide valuable insights into best practices and upcoming regulatory changes.

Furthermore, partnerships with other technology firms can facilitate knowledge sharing and collective compliance strategies. By fostering a culture of collaboration, businesses can create a robust compliance framework that not only meets regulatory requirements but also encourages innovation and growth.

Ultimately, compliance with industry standards in cloud computing is not merely a legal obligation but a strategic imperative. As businesses in China increasingly adopt cloud solutions, the ability to demonstrate compliance can differentiate them in a crowded market. IT and cloud professionals must prioritize compliance as a core component of their operational strategy, ensuring that their organizations are not only prepared to meet current standards but also agile enough to adapt to future regulatory changes. This proactive approach will position businesses for long-term success in the ever-evolving cloud computing landscape.

Lesson 4
ICP Filing and License

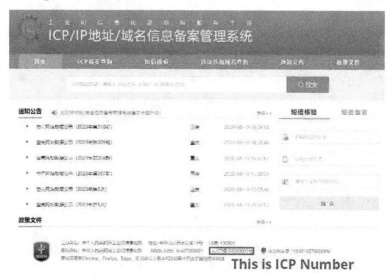

This is ICP Number

Establishing an online presence in China requires organizations to comply with a strict regulatory framework, one of the most critical elements being the Internet Content Provider (ICP) license. This mandatory certification, issued by the Ministry of Industry and Information Technology (MIIT), grants businesses the legal right to host and operate websites and online services on servers located within mainland China.

The ICP licensing system was introduced as part of China's broader internet governance policies, aimed at ensuring compliance with cybersecurity laws, content regulations, and data residency requirements. Websites that fail to obtain an ICP license risk being blocked by the Great Firewall, preventing access to users within China.

There are two main types of ICP certification:

1. ICP Filing (ICP Bei'An, ICP备案) – Required for non-commercial websites, such as informational sites, personal blogs, or corporate websites without direct online transactions.

2. ICP Commercial License (ICP Zheng, ICP证) – Mandatory for websites engaging in e-commerce, online payments, and other revenue-generating activities.

To obtain an ICP filing, organizations must submit an application detailing the nature of the website, its content, and the company's registration details. This process requires a Chinese business entity, a locally registered domain (.cn preferred), and hosting services within China. Foreign businesses without a legal presence in China typically partner with local companies or cloud providers like Alibaba Cloud, Tencent Cloud, or AWS China, which can assist in the filing process.

In addition to the basic ICP filing, businesses may also require additional permits depending on the nature of their online activities. For instance, companies involved in e-commerce or providing specific services may need to secure an ICP Commercial License.

This license allows for the monetization of online platforms and is subject to more stringent scrutiny. IT professionals must be aware of these requirements and ensure that their applications are comprehensive and cater to the specific needs of their business model within the Chinese context.

Maintaining compliance with ICP regulations does not end with obtaining the license. Once a website is operational, it is imperative to continuously monitor and manage content to align with the evolving legal landscape in China. Authorities periodically review websites to ensure adherence to regulations concerning content censorship and data privacy. Non-compliance can result in severe penalties, including fines or the suspension of services. Therefore, cloud professionals must implement robust content management strategies and stay informed about regulatory updates to mitigate risks.

Finally, the ICP process serves as a gateway for businesses to explore the vast opportunities presented by the Chinese cloud computing market. With the rapid growth of digital services in China, obtaining an ICP license not only legitimizes a company's online presence but also enhances its credibility among local consumers and partners.

By understanding and navigating the ICP licensing landscape, IT and business leaders can position their organizations strategically within one of the world's largest and most dynamic markets, ultimately driving growth and innovation in the cloud computing sector.

Lesson 5
Navigating Cross-Border Data Transfer Restrictions

Navigating cross-border data transfer restrictions is a critical aspect for businesses operating in the cloud computing landscape of China. As companies increasingly rely on global data flows to enhance operations and drive innovation, understanding the legal and regulatory frameworks governing these transfers is vital. China has established stringent data protection laws, particularly through the Cybersecurity Law (CSL) and the Personal Information Protection Law (PIPL), which impose specific requirements on how data can be collected, stored, and transferred outside of the country. IT and cloud professionals must be well-versed in these regulations to mitigate risks associated with non-compliance, which can lead to severe penalties and reputational damage.

One of the primary challenges in cross-border data transfers is the necessity for data localization. Under current Chinese laws, certain types of data, particularly personal information and important data, must be stored within Chinese territory. This requirement complicates the operational framework for businesses that rely on cloud services hosted in other countries. IT professionals need to assess their data classification and determine whether the information they handle falls under these localization mandates. Implementing robust data management strategies that prioritize local storage can help organizations comply with these regulations while maintaining operational efficiency.

Another crucial element of navigating cross-border restrictions is understanding the process of obtaining necessary permissions for data transfers. The PIPL outlines a series of conditions under which data may be transferred internationally, including the need for explicit consent from data subjects and the establishment of adequate protection measures for the data being transferred. Organizations must develop comprehensive data governance frameworks that include clear policies on consent management and risk assessments to ensure that they can legally transfer data across borders. This not only safeguards their operations but also builds trust with customers and partners. In addition to legal requirements, businesses must consider the technological and logistical implications of cross-border data transfers.

The infrastructure supporting cloud services must be capable of handling the complexities of data encryption, access controls, and auditing to ensure compliance with both local and international regulations. IT and cloud professionals should invest in advanced security technologies and practices that align with regulatory standards while also enhancing the overall resilience of their cloud environments. By integrating compliance into their technological strategy, organizations can better navigate the intricate landscape of data transfers.

However, even when compliance requirements are met, technical and political barriers further complicate cross-border data flows. The Great Firewall of China, the country's extensive system of internet censorship and monitoring, restricts access to foreign websites and slows down international connections. This poses a significant challenge for multinational companies that require seamless data exchange between China and global offices. Many organizations attempt to bypass these restrictions using Virtual Private Networks (VPNs), but China has strict laws against unauthorized VPN services. Government regulations mandate that only state-approved VPN providers can be legally used, meaning foreign companies must carefully evaluate their connectivity solutions to avoid potential legal and operational risks.

Lastly, staying abreast of the evolving regulatory landscape in China is essential for effective cross-border data management. As the country continues to refine its data protection laws and align them with global standards, organizations must remain vigilant and adaptable. Regular training and updates for IT staff, along with collaboration with legal experts, can help businesses remain compliant and responsive to changes in the regulatory environment. By proactively addressing these challenges, companies can not only protect themselves from potential legal pitfalls but also leverage their compliance efforts as a competitive advantage in the rapidly evolving cloud computing market in China.

Lesson 6
The Great Firewall of China

The Great Firewall of China (GFW) is the country's sophisticated internet censorship and surveillance system, designed to regulate and restrict access to foreign websites, online services, and data transfers. This system plays a crucial role in China's cyber sovereignty strategy, controlling information flow between China and the rest of the world while enforcing local regulations on internet content and data security.

For cloud professionals and multinational businesses, the Great Firewall presents several challenges when operating in China, particularly in areas such as:

- Restricted Access to Foreign Cloud Services – Many popular cloud platforms, SaaS applications, and developer tools (such as Google Cloud, Dropbox, and Slack) are inaccessible or face significant slowdowns.
- Reduced Internet Speed and Latency Issues – The filtering mechanisms of the Great Firewall cause high latency when accessing non-Chinese websites, making real-time data exchange difficult.
- Blocked APIs and Web Services – Many APIs used for global cloud applications may not function properly in China due to access restrictions, requiring local alternatives.
- Challenges in Data Synchronization and Remote Work – International companies struggle to sync data across borders, affecting workflows, collaboration tools, and real-time applications.

Despite these restrictions, businesses operating in China can take several strategic steps to minimize disruptions:

1. Hosting Within China: Deploying cloud infrastructure inside the country (e.g., AWS China, Alibaba Cloud, or Tencent Cloud) ensures compliance and significantly improves network performance.

2. Using Content Delivery Networks (CDNs): Leveraging Chinese CDNs (such as those provided by Alibaba, Tencent, or ChinaCache) can improve website and application performance while complying with regulations.

3. Localized Infrastructure for Applications: Companies should develop China-specific environments that separate operations from their global cloud setups.

4. Legal Cross-Border Connectivity Solutions: For companies that must transfer data internationally, state-approved solutions such as government-licensed VPNs and dedicated leased lines can help maintain compliance while ensuring connectivity.

Understanding the mechanics of the Great Firewall is crucial for businesses planning to establish a long-term presence in China. Companies must prioritize localization strategies and compliance measures to avoid legal repercussions while maintaining operational efficiency.

Lesson 7
VPN Restrictions in China

In many countries, Virtual Private Networks (VPNs) are commonly used to establish secure connections and bypass geo-restrictions. However, in China, VPN usage is heavily regulated, and unauthorized services are illegal.

The Cybersecurity Law (CSL) and Telecommunications Regulations classify unauthorized VPN usage as a violation of national cybersecurity policies. The government requires that:

- Only state-approved VPN providers can legally operate in China.
- Unauthorized VPNs are blocked by the Great Firewall, preventing users from accessing global content.
- Individuals and companies using unauthorized VPNs may face fines or legal consequences.
- Foreign businesses operating in China must work with government-licensed VPN providers to ensure compliance.

Many multinational companies rely on VPNs for secure cross-border communication, accessing foreign cloud services, and enabling remote work. However, VPN restrictions present several operational hurdles:

- Reduced Speed and Performance: Government filtering and monitoring cause unstable connections and slow VPN speeds.
- List item #2Risk of Non-Compliance: Unauthorized VPN use can jeopardize business operations, leading to penalties or service disruptions.
- Limited Access to Global Tools: Many essential business applications and SaaS services (e.g., Google Workspace, GitHub, and global cloud dashboards) remain inaccessible.

To ensure compliance while maintaining connectivity, companies can explore the following alternatives:

- Government-Approved VPNs: Businesses can apply for a licensed VPN through a local provider such as China Telecom or China Unicom.
- Dedicated Leased Lines: Multinational firms with high data transfer needs can establish dedicated international circuits, which are subject to government approval.
- Local Cloud Providers: Instead of routing through external VPNs, companies can host their services on Chinese cloud platforms to ensure better network performance.

By understanding and adhering to China's VPN regulations, companies can protect their operations while ensuring compliance with cybersecurity laws.

CHAPTER 3
CLOUD SERVICES PROVIDERS IN CHINA

Lesson 1
Introduction to the Competitive Landscape

The competitive landscape of cloud computing in China is characterized by a dynamic interplay of established industry giants and emerging startups. As the world's largest market for cloud services, China presents unique opportunities and challenges for IT professionals and business leaders alike. Understanding this landscape is crucial for stakeholders aiming to navigate the rapidly evolving technological environment. The state of competition is shaped by factors such as regulatory frameworks, technological advancements, and the growing demand for cloud solutions across various sectors.

Key players in the Chinese cloud computing market include domestic giants like Alibaba Cloud, Tencent Cloud, and Huawei Cloud, which have established significant market share and brand recognition. These companies have invested heavily in infrastructure and innovation, enabling them to offer a diverse range of services tailored to meet the needs of both small and large enterprises. Their ability to leverage vast amounts of data and advanced artificial intelligence capabilities positions them as formidable competitors, driving continuous improvements in service offerings and customer experiences.

Emerging startups are also making their mark on the competitive landscape. These nimble companies often focus on niche markets or innovative solutions that address specific pain points, allowing them to carve out unique positions in the industry. The agility of startups enables them to respond quickly to changing market demands and technological advancements, presenting a challenge to larger incumbents who may struggle with bureaucratic inertia. This diversity of competition fosters a vibrant ecosystem where new ideas can flourish, ultimately benefiting customers through increased choice and improved services.

Regulatory considerations play a significant role in shaping the competitive dynamics within the Chinese cloud computing sector. The government's emphasis on cybersecurity, data sovereignty, and compliance mandates influences how companies operate and compete.

IT professionals must stay informed about these regulations as they can impact everything from service delivery to data management practices. Understanding the regulatory landscape is essential for businesses looking to navigate compliance while optimizing their cloud strategies.

As the competition intensifies, collaboration and partnerships are becoming increasingly important. Companies are recognizing the value of working together to enhance their offerings and expand their reach. Strategic alliances, joint ventures, and ecosystem partnerships can provide the necessary resources and expertise to innovate and compete effectively in this fast-paced market. For IT and cloud professionals, embracing a collaborative mindset can open up new avenues for growth and success in the evolving landscape of cloud computing in China.

Lesson 2
AWS China

AWS China plays a pivotal role in the country's cloud computing ecosystem, offering a localized version of Amazon Web Services (AWS) that aligns with China's regulatory, operational, and business landscape. Unlike its global counterpart, AWS China operates independently due to strict government regulations, requiring localized partnerships, compliance frameworks, and infrastructure tailored to the Chinese market.

AWS first entered China in 2013, but unlike other regions where AWS operates directly, the Chinese government mandates that cloud service providers partner with local companies. As a result, AWS China runs its services through two independent partners: Sinnet, which operates the AWS China (Beijing) Region, and Northwest Cloud Data (NWCD), which manages the AWS China (Ningxia) Region. These partnerships ensure compliance with China's Cybersecurity Law and data localization mandates, which require that all cloud operations and customer data remain within Chinese borders.

While AWS China offers a comprehensive suite of cloud services, including computing, storage, AI, and networking, it differs significantly from AWS Global. The most notable distinction is its isolated infrastructure, which means that AWS China operates in a completely separate environment from AWS Global, with no direct connectivity between its regions and AWS's global network. Regulatory compliance is another major differentiator, as customers must navigate additional licensing and compliance requirements, including the ICP filing for internet-facing services. Additionally, while AWS China provides most core cloud services, certain advanced offerings such as AWS Global Accelerator, SageMaker, and some AI services may be delayed or unavailable due to regulatory constraints. AWS China also follows a separate billing structure, which varies between Sinnet and NWCD, unlike AWS Global's unified pay-as-you-go pricing model. Despite these differences, many multinational corporations and local enterprises choose AWS China for its reliability, security, and extensive service portfolio. Businesses operating in highly regulated industries, such as finance, healthcare, and e-commerce, rely on AWS China's compliance-ready infrastructure to meet China's strict data security laws.

AWS China also provides enterprise-grade infrastructure, ensuring high availability and low latency through multiple availability zones across Beijing and Ningxia. The platform's robust suite of AI, machine learning, IoT, and analytics tools enables companies to accelerate innovation while reducing operational complexity. Additionally, AWS China supports hybrid and multi-cloud environments, allowing enterprises to integrate AWS with local cloud providers such as Alibaba Cloud or Tencent Cloud for optimized workload distribution.

AWS China currently operates in two main cloud regions: AWS China (Beijing), managed by Sinnet, and AWS China (Ningxia), managed by NWCD. The Beijing region serves as a primary hub for businesses in Northern China, including financial institutions, government agencies, and AI-driven enterprises. Meanwhile, the Ningxia region is widely used in manufacturing, logistics, and energy sectors, offering scalable and secure cloud solutions. Both regions provide multiple availability zones (AZs), ensuring fault-tolerant and high-performing applications.

Lesson 3
Azure China

Azure China is a vital component of China's cloud computing ecosystem, providing a localized version of Microsoft's cloud platform that complies with China's unique regulatory, operational, and business landscape. Unlike its global counterpart, Azure China operates as an independent cloud environment, governed by China's strict cybersecurity and data localization laws, requiring local partnerships and infrastructure tailored to Chinese regulations.

Microsoft first introduced Azure in China in 2014, but due to the country's legal requirements, the company does not operate Azure directly. Instead, Azure China runs through two independent partners: 21Vianet, which operates the Azure China regions, and Shanghai Blue Cloud, a subsidiary of 21Vianet that ensures localization and compliance. These partnerships allow Azure to maintain regulatory approval, ensuring that data, infrastructure, and cloud services fully comply with China's Cybersecurity Law and data sovereignty regulations, which mandate that all cloud operations and customer data remain within Chinese borders.

While Azure China offers a comprehensive suite of cloud services, including virtual machines, databases, AI, analytics, and enterprise solutions, it differs significantly from Azure Global. The most notable distinction is its isolated infrastructure, meaning that Azure China operates as a completely separate environment from Azure Global, with no direct integration between China's regions and Microsoft's global cloud network. Another key difference is regulatory compliance, as companies deploying cloud workloads in China must navigate additional licensing and compliance processes, including ICP registration for public-facing services. Additionally, while Azure China provides core cloud services, certain advanced features such as Azure OpenAI, Power Automate, and specific hybrid cloud solutions may be delayed or unavailable due to China's regulatory landscape. Azure China also follows a different billing model, requiring customers to work with 21Vianet for pricing and support rather than Microsoft's global billing system.

Despite these differences, Azure China remains a top choice for enterprises looking for a scalable, secure, and compliance-driven cloud solution in China. Businesses operating in highly regulated industries, such as finance, healthcare, manufacturing, and government sectors, rely on Azure China's security-first approach to meet local compliance requirements while leveraging Microsoft's trusted cloud ecosystem. Azure China also provides enterprise-grade infrastructure, ensuring high availability and low latency through its multiple availability zones. Its AI, IoT, big data, and enterprise application services empower companies to accelerate innovation while maintaining compliance with China's strict cloud computing policies. Additionally, Azure China is widely used in hybrid and multi-cloud environments, allowing companies to integrate Microsoft cloud solutions with Alibaba Cloud, Tencent Cloud, or Huawei Cloud to optimize their workloads.

Azure China currently operates in multiple cloud regions, all managed by 21Vianet: Azure China North (Beijing and nearby regions) Serving government agencies, financial institutions, and AI-driven enterprises in Northern China. Azure China East (Shanghai and surrounding regions), Primarily supporting technology, manufacturing, and retail industries. Each region consists of multiple availability zones (AZs), providing businesses with scalability, redundancy, and resilience for their cloud workloads. These regions also ensure that organizations comply with China's data localization requirements, preventing data from being transferred outside of China.

Lesson 4
Alibaba Cloud

Alibaba Cloud, also known as Aliyun, is the largest cloud service provider in China and a key player in the global cloud computing industry. As China's leading cloud platform, Alibaba Cloud has been instrumental in powering businesses, government agencies, and startups, offering a localized cloud environment that aligns with China's regulatory, operational, and business landscape. Unlike its international competitors, Alibaba Cloud benefits from deep integration with China's digital ecosystem, leveraging its parent company Alibaba Group's dominance in e-commerce, finance, and AI-driven cloud solutions.

Founded in 2009, Alibaba Cloud rapidly expanded to become the dominant cloud provider in China, surpassing competitors in market share, service offerings, and infrastructure scale. Unlike foreign cloud providers operating in China under government-imposed restrictions, Alibaba Cloud operates independently, making it the go-to choice for businesses needing seamless cloud integration within China. The company has also expanded globally, providing cloud solutions across Asia, Europe, the Middle East, and North America.

While Alibaba Cloud offers a comprehensive range of cloud services, including computing, storage, AI, analytics, and security solutions, it differs from AWS, Azure, and Tencent Cloud in several key ways. Its ecosystem is highly optimized for China, meaning that many cloud-native applications, developer tools, and enterprise solutions are designed specifically for the Chinese market. Another key differentiator is its tight integration with Alibaba Group's digital platforms, including Taobao, Tmall, Alipay, and Cainiao, providing businesses with powerful analytics, AI-driven e-commerce solutions, and supply chain optimizations. Alibaba Cloud also follows a different security and compliance model, aligning with China's Cybersecurity Law and Multi-Level Protection Scheme (MLPS) to ensure full regulatory compliance for data sovereignty and localization. Despite its dominance, companies choose Alibaba Cloud not just for its market leadership, but also for its high-performance infrastructure and enterprise solutions. The platform is widely used in industries such as e-commerce, finance, healthcare, gaming, and logistics, supporting businesses with cutting-edge AI, machine learning, and IoT solutions.

Alibaba Cloud also provides one of the most extensive hybrid and multi-cloud environments, allowing businesses to connect their workloads with AWS, Azure, and Tencent Cloud while remaining compliant with Chinese regulations.

Alibaba Cloud currently operates the largest cloud infrastructure in China, with multiple cloud regions and availability zones spread across the country. The primary cloud regions include: Alibaba Cloud China North (Beijing and Hebei), Catering to government agencies, AI research, and finance enterprises in Northern China. Alibaba Cloud China East (Shanghai and Jiangsu) Supporting manufacturing, retail, and technology companies with low-latency and high-performance computing solutions. Alibaba Cloud China South (Shenzhen and Guangdong). A hub for gaming, fintech, and logistics services, optimized for cross-border trade and cloud-based mobile applications. Each region includes multiple availability zones (AZs), ensuring businesses achieve scalability, security, and high availability for mission-critical workloads. Additionally, Alibaba Cloud operates dedicated government cloud regions, allowing state-owned enterprises and public sector organizations to leverage cloud computing under strict national security regulations.

Lesson 5
Huawei Cloud

Huawei Cloud is one of China's leading cloud service providers, offering a fully localized cloud computing environment tailored to China's regulatory, operational, and business landscape. As a subsidiary of Huawei Technologies, Huawei Cloud has established itself as a dominant force in the Chinese cloud market, competing directly with Alibaba Cloud, Tencent Cloud, and international players such as AWS and Azure China. Its deep integration with Huawei's enterprise technology ecosystem makes it a preferred choice for government agencies, telecom providers, AI-driven industries, and large enterprises seeking a secure and compliant cloud solution in China.

Launched in 2017, Huawei Cloud has rapidly grown into one of the top cloud providers in China, leveraging Huawei's expertise in network infrastructure, 5G, and AI computing. Unlike foreign cloud providers that operate in China under government-imposed restrictions, Huawei Cloud operates natively within China's regulated cloud ecosystem. Its strong government and enterprise partnerships have allowed it to expand aggressively, becoming a key player in both the Chinese and global cloud markets.

While Huawei Cloud offers a comprehensive range of cloud services, including computing, storage, AI, analytics, and security solutions, it differentiates itself from AWS, Azure, and Alibaba Cloud in several key ways. One of its biggest strengths is its integration with Huawei's telecommunications and 5G networks, making it the leading choice for cloud solutions in telecom, smart cities, and AI-driven industries. Huawei Cloud also follows a unique security and compliance model, aligning with China's Cybersecurity Law and Multi-Level Protection Scheme (MLPS) to ensure full regulatory compliance for data sovereignty and localization.

Many enterprises choose Huawei Cloud not just for its technological innovations but also for its secure, enterprise-grade infrastructure and AI-powered solutions. The platform is widely used across finance, healthcare, manufacturing, and AI research, providing cutting-edge AI, machine learning, and IoT services.

Huawei Cloud is also a leader in hybrid and multi-cloud solutions, enabling businesses to seamlessly integrate workloads across Alibaba Cloud, Tencent Cloud, and international providers while ensuring full compliance with Chinese regulations.

Huawei Cloud operates an extensive cloud infrastructure across China, with multiple availability zones and dedicated enterprise cloud regions. The primary cloud regions include: Huawei Cloud China North (Beijing and Inner Mongolia), Serving government agencies, AI research labs, and financial enterprises. Huawei Cloud China East (Shanghai and Suzhou), Optimized for manufacturing, e-commerce, and enterprise cloud computing. Huawei Cloud China South (Guangzhou and Shenzhen). A hub for telecom services, gaming, and AI-driven cloud applications. Each region includes multiple availability zones (AZs) to ensure scalability, redundancy, and low-latency performance. Huawei Cloud is also widely used in government-backed smart city initiatives, leveraging 5G, edge computing, and AI to enhance urban infrastructure, public services, and security.

Lesson 6
Tencent Cloud

Tencent Cloud is one of China's top cloud service providers, offering a fully localized cloud ecosystem that caters to the country's regulatory, operational, and business landscape. As a subsidiary of Tencent Holdings, the technology giant behind WeChat, QQ, and a vast gaming empire, Tencent Cloud is a dominant player in the Chinese cloud market, competing directly with Alibaba Cloud, Huawei Cloud, and global providers such as AWS and Azure China. Its strong presence in gaming, media, fintech, and AI-driven applications makes it a preferred choice for digital businesses, multinational corporations, and AI enterprises seeking a secure and compliant cloud infrastructure in China.

Founded in 2010, Tencent Cloud has grown into a leading cloud provider, leveraging Tencent's expertise in social media, gaming, and AI computing. Unlike foreign cloud providers that operate in China under government-imposed restrictions, Tencent Cloud operates natively within China's regulated cloud ecosystem, benefiting from strategic partnerships with government agencies, financial institutions, and tech enterprises. It has also expanded globally, with data centers across Asia, North America, and Europe, serving multinational clients.

While Tencent Cloud offers a comprehensive range of cloud services, including computing, storage, AI, analytics, and security solutions, it differentiates itself from AWS, Azure, Alibaba Cloud, and Huawei Cloud in several ways. One of its biggest strengths is its dominance in China's gaming and entertainment industry, providing cloud solutions for game developers, media streaming services, and social platforms. Tencent Cloud also follows a unique security and compliance model, aligning with China's Cybersecurity Law and Multi-Level Protection Scheme (MLPS) to ensure full regulatory compliance for data sovereignty and localization.

Many enterprises choose Tencent Cloud not just for its technological innovations, but also for its high-performance infrastructure, AI-powered cloud services, and seamless integration with Tencent's digital platforms.

The platform is widely used in industries such as gaming, fintech, social media, and AI research, providing cutting-edge machine learning, big data, and IoT solutions. Tencent Cloud is also a major player in hybrid and multi-cloud strategies, enabling businesses to connect workloads across Alibaba Cloud, Huawei Cloud, and international providers while ensuring full compliance with Chinese regulations.

Tencent Cloud operates an extensive cloud infrastructure across China, with multiple availability zones and dedicated enterprise cloud regions. The primary cloud regions include: Tencent Cloud China North (Beijing and Tianjin), Serving government agencies, AI research labs, and financial enterprises. Tencent Cloud China East (Shanghai and Jiangsu), Optimized for e-commerce, manufacturing, and enterprise cloud computing. Tencent Cloud China South (Guangzhou and Shenzhen). A hub for gaming, fintech, and AI-driven cloud applications, supporting Tencent's WeChat ecosystem, online banking, and digital payments. Each region includes multiple availability zones (AZs) to ensure scalability, redundancy, and low-latency performance. Tencent Cloud is also a leader in smart city solutions, providing cloud-based AI, security, and 5G connectivity to enhance urban infrastructure, transportation, and digital governance.

Lesson 7
Other Cloud Providers in China

While Alibaba Cloud, Huawei Cloud, Tencent Cloud, AWS China, and Azure China dominate the Chinese cloud computing landscape, several other providers contribute to the industry's rapid expansion. These cloud platforms offer specialized services, target niche markets, and play a crucial role in China's evolving digital economy.

Baidu Cloud, also known as Baidu AI Cloud, is one of China's leading cloud platforms, leveraging Baidu's expertise in artificial intelligence, big data, and autonomous driving technologies. Unlike Alibaba Cloud and Tencent Cloud, which focus on enterprise solutions and e-commerce ecosystems, Baidu Cloud is deeply integrated with AI research, natural language processing, and cloud-based machine learning services. It is widely used in autonomous vehicle development, smart cities, and AI-driven applications. With a 9% market share, Baidu Cloud continues to grow, particularly in industries that require high-performance AI and data analytics solutions.

China Telecom, one of the largest state-owned telecom operators, offers e-Cloud, a cloud platform specializing in government projects, public sector cloud infrastructure, and telecom-driven cloud solutions. Its deep integration with China's 5G networks allows e-Cloud to provide low-latency computing, edge cloud services, and IoT connectivity for smart cities and industrial applications. While e-Cloud does not compete directly with Alibaba Cloud or Huawei Cloud in the commercial cloud market, it plays a vital role in China's digital infrastructure strategy, supporting state-backed cloud initiatives.

China Mobile, China's largest telecommunications provider, operates China Mobile Cloud, a cloud platform designed to support 5G networks, enterprise cloud computing, and mobile internet applications. With China's aggressive push toward digitalization and 5G expansion, China Mobile Cloud is increasingly being used by telecom companies, financial services firms, and public institutions that require secure, scalable cloud solutions. The platform's tight integration with China Mobile's nationwide network infrastructure makes it a preferred choice for organizations needing fast, reliable cloud connectivity.

JD Cloud, operated by JD.com, specializes in e-commerce-driven cloud services, supply chain optimization, and AI-enhanced logistics solutions. Unlike Alibaba Cloud, which caters to a broad range of industries, JD Cloud focuses primarily on retail, warehousing, and data-driven e-commerce applications. It provides cloud-based smart retail solutions, real-time logistics tracking, and AI-driven customer engagement tools. JD Cloud is an attractive choice for businesses seeking cloud services specifically optimized for China's e-commerce ecosystem.

Kingsoft Cloud is one of China's fastest-growing independent cloud providers, offering cloud computing solutions tailored to gaming, multimedia, and enterprise applications. Unlike its competitors, which focus heavily on infrastructure as a service (IaaS), Kingsoft Cloud has made a name for itself in content delivery networks (CDNs), cloud storage, and cloud-based gaming services. It is widely used in video streaming, mobile applications, and software development, making it a popular choice for China's digital entertainment industry.

CHAPTER 4
ARCHITECTING CLOUD SOLUTIONS IN CHINA

Lesson 1
Building a Scalable Cloud Infrastructure

Building a scalable cloud infrastructure in China requires a unique approach that takes into account regulatory requirements, provider-specific constraints, and the fragmented cloud market. Unlike other regions where businesses can deploy cloud services seamlessly across different providers and geographies, China presents a distinct set of challenges that must be carefully navigated. Strict compliance laws, localized cloud ecosystems, and geopolitical factors make scalability in China a strategic endeavor, requiring companies to carefully design, optimize, and manage their cloud environments.

China's cloud market operates differently from the rest of the world. Foreign cloud providers such as AWS and Azure cannot operate independently and must form joint ventures with local companies to comply with government regulations. This has led to the emergence of a highly localized market, where Alibaba Cloud, Huawei Cloud, Tencent Cloud, Baidu Cloud, and China Telecom Cloud dominate the landscape.

The geographic and regulatory isolation of China's cloud infrastructure means that global cloud regions do not seamlessly integrate with Chinese regions. Companies that need scalability across both Chinese and global markets must carefully architect hybrid and multi-cloud solutions to ensure operational efficiency and compliance.

Additionally, businesses must consider how the regulatory landscape affects scalability. Expanding cloud services in China is not just a matter of provisioning new resources—it requires ICP filings, security audits, and compliance with China's Cybersecurity Law, all of which impact how quickly and efficiently companies can scale their infrastructure.

Lesson 2
Scaling Strategies for Cloud Deployments in China

1. Selecting the Right Cloud Provider for Scalability

Unlike in many global markets where companies can standardize on AWS or Azure, businesses in China often require a multi-cloud or hybrid approach. The choice of cloud provider plays a critical role in scalability, as different providers offer distinct advantages depending on the industry, data requirements, and regulatory considerations.

- Alibaba Cloud is the largest cloud provider in China, widely used for e-commerce, AI, and enterprise cloud solutions. It offers deep integration with China's digital economy and is often the preferred choice for businesses operating within Alibaba's ecosystem.
- Huawei Cloud is rapidly expanding in AI, telecommunications, and government-backed projects. It is an attractive choice for companies leveraging 5G, smart city solutions, or AI-driven applications.
- Tencent Cloud is heavily focused on gaming, fintech, and media services, making it ideal for companies that require high-performance computing for entertainment platforms.
- AWS China & Azure China are strategic choices for multinational corporations seeking global consistency in cloud operations. These platforms offer a familiar cloud environment but require compliance with local regulatory requirements.

The provider selection process is crucial because switching providers later can be costly and time-consuming, especially when dealing with data migration restrictions and compliance approvals.

2. Multi-Region Deployments for Scalability

Unlike in North America or Europe, where a single cloud region can serve an entire continent, China's cloud regions are geographically isolated.

Companies must strategically distribute their workloads across multiple cloud regions to ensure low latency, high availability, and disaster recovery capabilities.

For scalability, businesses should deploy resources across multiple availability zones (AZs) in key economic hubs, such as:

- North China (Beijing, Tianjin) – Ideal for financial institutions, AI research, and government cloud projects.
- East China (Shanghai, Suzhou, Hangzhou) – Best suited for manufacturing, e-commerce, and enterprise applications.
- South China (Shenzhen, Guangzhou, Hong Kong) – A hub for gaming, fintech, cross-border trade, and logistics cloud solutions.

A multi-region deployment strategy ensures that businesses can serve customers efficiently across China's diverse geography, reducing latency and enhancing the scalability of cloud workloads.

3. Regulatory Compliance as a Scalability Constraint

Scaling cloud operations in China is not just a technical challenge—it's a compliance challenge. Unlike in Western markets, where businesses can scale cloud services at will, China imposes legal and regulatory hurdles that must be cleared before cloud services can be expanded. Some of the key compliance factors that impact scalability include:

- ICP Licensing: Companies operating public-facing applications in China must obtain an Internet Content Provider (ICP) license before launching or scaling services. Without this approval, businesses risk being blocked by the Great Firewall.
- Data Residency Requirements: China's Cybersecurity Law mandates that certain categories of data (including personal and business-critical information) must be stored within Chinese borders, preventing companies from scaling globally without additional approvals.
- Security Audits (MLPS 2.0): Organizations handling sensitive customer data must undergo security classification audits to ensure compliance with China's Multi-Level Protection Scheme (MLPS 2.0). This process can delay cloud expansion and requires ongoing compliance management.

To scale effectively, businesses must anticipate compliance challenges early and work with local legal experts and cloud partners to streamline the approval process.

4. Automating and Managing a Scalable Cloud Environment

Given the complexity of managing cloud operations across multiple regions and providers, automation plays a critical role in ensuring efficient scaling. Businesses expanding their cloud footprint in China should leverage:

- Cloud-native automation tools such as Alibaba Cloud Resource Orchestration Service (ROS), Huawei Cloud CloudOps, and Tencent Cloud TStack to manage multi-cloud deployments.
- Multi-cloud monitoring platforms to provide a unified dashboard for infrastructure management across different providers.
- AI-driven auto-scaling to dynamically adjust computing resources in response to real-time traffic spikes, particularly for businesses in e-commerce, gaming, and financial services.

An effective cloud automation strategy allows businesses to scale efficiently while reducing operational complexity and compliance risks.

Lesson 3
Best Practices for High Availability and Disaster Recovery in China

Ensuring high availability (HA) and disaster recovery (DR) in China's unique cloud computing environment requires a customized approach that accounts for the country's regulatory constraints, regional network fragmentation, and cloud provider-specific capabilities. Unlike in other global markets where businesses can seamlessly distribute workloads across multiple cloud regions, China's geopolitical, regulatory, and infrastructure-specific challenges demand tailored HA/DR strategies to minimize disruptions and ensure business continuity.

1.Selecting the Right Cloud Provider for HA/DR

Not all cloud providers in China offer the same level of high availability and disaster recovery solutions. Businesses must carefully select cloud providers based on industry needs and compliance requirements:

- Alibaba Cloud: Offers multi-region failover, cross-region backup services, and active geo-redundancy solutions for large-scale enterprises.
- Huawei Cloud: Strong in AI-driven disaster recovery, particularly for telecommunications, government agencies, and finance.
- Tencent Cloud: Provides game industry-specific HA/DR solutions, including real-time failover for high-traffic applications.
- AWS China & Azure China: Best suited for multinational enterprises, but require strict data residency compliance and localized backup storage.

2. Implementing Multi-Region Failover Strategies

Given China's regional cloud isolation, businesses should:

- Deploy resources in at least three major cloud regions (e.g., Beijing, Shanghai, Shenzhen) to ensure geographic redundancy.

- Use cloud-native failover solutions such as Alibaba Cloud's PolarDB Multi-Zone HA and Huawei Cloud's Geo-Disaster Recovery Service.
- Configure automated database replication and asynchronous backups across multiple availability zones (AZs).

3. Leveraging Edge Computing for Real-Time HA/DR

For businesses operating in industries such as e-commerce, fintech, and manufacturing, leveraging edge computing can improve high availability and disaster recovery performance.

- Deploy content delivery networks (CDNs) such as Alibaba Cloud CDN or ChinaCache to reduce downtime in the event of cloud failure.
- Use edge cloud storage to store temporary failover data closer to end users, ensuring seamless continuity of service during outages.

4. Ensuring Regulatory Compliance for Disaster Recovery

China's Multi-Level Protection Scheme (MLPS 2.0) requires businesses to implement security protocols for data protection and failover systems.

- Regularly test disaster recovery plans to ensure compliance with MLPS 2.0 standards.
- Encrypt cross-region backups and limit access based on China's cybersecurity requirements.

Lesson 4
Networking and CDN Solutions in China

Expanding a digital presence in China presents unique networking and content delivery challenges that businesses do not typically encounter in other regions. Due to China's unique internet architecture, regulatory constraints, and fragmented connectivity, companies must adapt their networking and CDN strategies to ensure low-latency, high-availability services while remaining compliant with local laws. Unlike in global markets where businesses can rely on a single cloud provider's backbone network, China's isolated internet infrastructure and regional network inconsistencies require a tailored approach to networking and content delivery.

Unlike in North America or Europe, where the internet operates as a highly interconnected global network, China's internet infrastructure is heavily regulated, regionally fragmented, and controlled by state-owned telecommunications providers. The three primary internet service providers (ISPs) in China. China Telecom, China Unicom, and China Mobile each operate semi-independent networks that do not always interconnect efficiently. As a result, businesses expanding to China must carefully design their network architecture to avoid performance bottlenecks.

1. The Impact of the Great Firewall on Networking

The Great Firewall of China (GFW) is a nationwide internet filtering system that regulates cross-border internet traffic. While its primary function is censorship, it also affects network performance in several key ways:

- Increased Latency: International connections between China and the rest of the world suffer from higher latency due to deep packet inspection and content filtering.
- Unpredictable Routing: Some websites and applications experience inconsistent access speeds depending on user location and network conditions.

- Cross-Border Data Restrictions: Businesses cannot rely on foreign-hosted infrastructure for serving content within China without significant performance degradation or outright blocking.

To mitigate these issues, companies expanding into China should:

- Host infrastructure within China, leveraging local cloud providers (Alibaba Cloud, Huawei Cloud, Tencent Cloud) rather than relying on global AWS or Azure regions.
- Use state-approved cross-border connectivity solutions such as China Telecom's MPLS VPNs or dedicated leased lines for critical business applications.
- Ensure compliance with content and data regulations to prevent disruptions caused by the Great Firewall's content filtering mechanisms.

As organizations in China continue to embrace digital transformation, the importance of effective networking and CDN solutions will only grow. IT and cloud professionals must stay abreast of technological advancements and market trends to optimize their strategies. By leveraging the right networking tools and CDN capabilities, businesses can enhance their operational efficiency, improve user engagement, and maintain a competitive edge in the fast-evolving landscape of cloud computing in China.

2. Why CDNs Are Essential for China

Given China's regionalized network structure, Content Delivery Networks (CDNs) play a critical role in improving performance, reliability, and accessibility. Without a well-optimized CDN strategy, businesses will struggle with slow-loading websites, unreliable application performance, and degraded user experience.

Unlike in other markets, where a single data center or cloud region can effectively serve an entire country, China's network fragmentation and regional infrastructure inconsistencies require businesses to distribute their content strategically. CDNs help mitigate these challenges by:

- Reducing Latency: By caching content closer to end users, CDNs minimize load times and improve responsiveness.
- Overcoming ISP Fragmentation: Since China's ISPs operate semi-independently, CDN networks ensure consistent access speeds across different provinces and regions.

- Ensuring Regulatory Compliance: Hosting content inside China via local CDN providers helps businesses comply with ICP licensing requirements and avoid Great Firewall disruptions.

3. Selecting the Right CDN Provider in China

Several local CDN providers dominate the market, each offering solutions optimized for specific industries and content types:

- Alibaba Cloud CDN: Best suited for e-commerce platforms, media streaming services, and enterprise websites looking to optimize low-latency content delivery within China.
- Tencent Cloud CDN: A leading choice for gaming companies, mobile applications, and video content platforms, leveraging Tencent's ecosystem and AI-powered content acceleration.
- Huawei Cloud CDN: Ideal for enterprise SaaS platforms and AI-driven applications, offering deep integration with Huawei's edge computing and IoT solutions.
- ChinaCache: A long-established Chinese CDN provider specializing in high-performance caching solutions for financial services, logistics, and enterprise applications.

4. Managing Cross-Border Connectivity Issues

Since international network connections are slow and unreliable, businesses with global operations must design a China-specific networking strategy that includes:

- Deploying a Hybrid Cloud Model: Combining on-premises resources, a China-based cloud provider, and a global cloud service to maintain operational flexibility.
- Using Dedicated Cross-Border Connectivity Services: China Telecom and China Unicom offer state-approved VPNs, MPLS connections, and leased lines to improve cross-border data flow.
- Ensuring Legal Compliance: Businesses must obtain official approval for cross-border data transfers, especially if handling personal or financial data.

5. Regulatory Compliance for Content Hosting and Delivery

Hosting content in China requires compliance with strict content regulations. Businesses must:

- Obtain an ICP License: Any website serving content in China must have an ICP Filing or ICP Commercial License, which is mandatory for using local CDNs.
- Ensure Content Filtering Compliance: The Great Firewall actively blocks certain keywords, topics, and foreign-hosted content, requiring localized content strategies.
- Work with Government-Approved CDN Providers: To avoid disruptions, businesses should rely on CDNs operated by approved Chinese companies (e.g., Alibaba Cloud, Tencent Cloud, Baidu Cloud).

6. Optimizing Performance Across China's Network Infrastructure

To deliver a high-performance experience to users across China, businesses should:

- Use Edge Computing Solutions: Deploy localized edge nodes in high-density urban centers to process user requests faster.
- Leverage AI-Driven Traffic Routing: Alibaba Cloud and Tencent Cloud offer intelligent traffic routing services that dynamically optimize network paths to reduce latency.
- Monitor Network Performance Continuously: Real-time analytics help detect bottlenecks and optimize traffic distribution across different network providers.

CHAPTER 5
OPTIMIZING CLOUD OPERATIONS IN CHINA

Lesson 1
Cost Management and Optimization

Managing cloud costs in China requires a localized approach, as pricing structures, regulatory costs, and infrastructure constraints differ significantly from global markets. Unlike in North America or Europe, where cloud services are standardized, China's cloud ecosystem is dominated by local providers, each with unique pricing models, government incentives, and regional pricing variations. Additionally, data sovereignty laws, high cross-border data transfer costs, and compliance-driven expenses add complexity to cost optimization.

1. Pricing Variations Across Cloud Providers and Regions

The cost of cloud services varies depending on the provider, region, and type of workload:

- Alibaba Cloud and Tencent Cloud generally offer more competitive pricing than AWS China and Azure China, especially for compute and storage resources.
- Hosting in Tier-1 cities (Beijing, Shanghai) is significantly more expensive than in Ningxia or Inner Mongolia, where government incentives and lower energy costs reduce cloud expenses.
- State-backed providers like China Telecom Cloud offer discounted rates for strategic industries, including AI, manufacturing, and fintech.

2. Compliance-Driven Costs

Unlike in Western markets, compliance costs in China can be a major expense:

- ICP Licensing: Any public-facing cloud deployment requires an Internet Content Provider (ICP) license, which can involve legal and administrative fees.
- MLPS 2.0 Security Audits: Businesses handling sensitive data must comply with Multi-Level Protection Scheme (MLPS 2.0) regulations, often requiring additional security investments.

- Data Residency Laws: Transferring data out of China is expensive and tightly regulated, making cross-border data transfer a cost factor businesses must plan for.

3. Managing Cloud Spending with FinOps

To control cloud costs, companies operating in China should adopt FinOps (Cloud Financial Operations) strategies:

- Monitor and optimize workloads using local cost-management tools (e.g., Alibaba Cloud Cost Center, Tencent Cloud Billing Reports).
- Use reserved instances and long-term contracts to secure discounted pricing.
- Implement budget alerts and governance policies to prevent overspending, especially when working with multiple cloud providers.

4. Optimizing Multi-Cloud and Hybrid Strategies

Due to China's fragmented cloud market, businesses often use multiple providers to balance costs and performance:

- Deploying core workloads on cost-effective local clouds (Alibaba, Huawei, Tencent) while using AWS China or Azure China for global consistency.
- Reducing data transfer costs by keeping processing and storage within China, minimizing outbound traffic fees.
- Leveraging government incentives in lower-cost regions for compute-intensive workloads.

Lesson 2
Local Talent and Support

The growth of cloud computing in China has been significantly influenced by the local talent pool and the support systems established to nurture innovation and development in this sector. As IT professionals and business leaders navigate the complexities of this rapidly evolving landscape, understanding the dynamics of local talent becomes essential. China boasts a large number of graduates in science, technology, engineering, and mathematics (STEM) fields, with many specializing in cloud computing technologies. This influx of skilled workers provides the foundation for robust cloud infrastructure and services, enabling companies to harness local expertise for competitive advantage.

In addition to a well-educated workforce, various initiatives and programs by the Chinese government are enhancing the viability of local talent in the cloud computing area. The government has invested heavily in education and training programs aimed at upskilling professionals in emerging technologies. These initiatives often focus on cloud computing, artificial intelligence, and big data, ensuring that the workforce is well-equipped to meet the demands of the industry. Furthermore, partnerships between educational institutions and technology companies foster hands-on experience, bridging the gap between theoretical knowledge and practical application.

Support for local talent also extends to incubators and accelerators that have emerged across major Chinese cities. These organizations provide essential resources, mentorship, and networking opportunities for startups and entrepreneurs in the cloud sector. By creating an ecosystem that promotes collaboration, these incubators facilitate the sharing of ideas and resources, ultimately leading to the development of innovative cloud solutions. As startups gain traction, they contribute to the overall growth of the cloud computing market in China, attracting further investment and interest from both local and international stakeholders.

The role of local talent is not just limited to technical expertise; it also encompasses the cultural understanding required to navigate the unique business environment in China. Professionals with local insights can help foreign companies adapt their strategies to align with regional practices and consumer preferences.

This cultural competence is critical for successful market entry and sustained growth, as cloud computing solutions must often be tailored to meet the specific needs of Chinese businesses and consumers. By leveraging local talent, organizations can enhance their market positioning and achieve long-term success in the competitive landscape.

As the cloud computing sector in China continues to mature, the interplay between local talent and support systems will remain pivotal. IT and cloud professionals, along with business leaders, must actively engage in nurturing this talent through mentorship, training, and collaboration. By fostering a culture of innovation and continuous learning, organizations can not only enhance their capabilities but also contribute to the overall advancement of the cloud computing industry in China. The synergy between local talent and supportive ecosystems is poised to drive future growth, ensuring that China remains a key player in the global cloud computing landscape.

CHAPTER 6
EMERGING TECHNOLOGIESAND TRENDS

Lesson 1
AI and Machine Learning in the Cloud

The integration of artificial intelligence (AI) and machine learning (ML) into cloud computing has revolutionized the way businesses operate in China. As the country continues to accelerate its digital transformation, enterprises are increasingly leveraging cloud-based AI and ML solutions to enhance their capabilities. The combination of vast data storage, processing power, and advanced algorithms available in the cloud allows organizations to gain insights that were previously unattainable. This synergy not only fosters innovation but also drives efficiency, enabling businesses to remain competitive in a rapidly evolving market.

One of the critical advantages of using AI and ML in the cloud is the scalability these technologies offer. Traditional on-premises solutions often face limitations in terms of infrastructure and resource allocation. In contrast, cloud platforms provide on-demand access to computational power, allowing organizations to scale their AI and ML applications according to their needs. This flexibility is particularly crucial for businesses in China, where market dynamics can change swiftly. By utilizing cloud resources, companies can quickly adapt their models and algorithms to meet new challenges or capitalize on emerging opportunities.

Data is the lifeblood of AI and ML, and the cloud serves as an ideal environment for data management and analysis. Chinese enterprises are generating immense volumes of data daily, and cloud platforms are equipped to handle this influx. With advanced data storage solutions and analytics tools, businesses can efficiently collect, store, and process data to train their AI models. Furthermore, the cloud facilitates collaboration among teams and departments, enabling them to share insights and findings seamlessly. This collaborative approach enhances the quality of AI applications and accelerates the deployment of innovative solutions. Security and compliance remain paramount concerns for organizations utilizing AI and ML in the cloud. As businesses in China navigate stringent regulations surrounding data privacy and protection, cloud service providers are stepping up their efforts to ensure compliance. Leading cloud platforms offer robust security measures, including encryption, access controls, and continuous monitoring, to safeguard sensitive data.

These features not only help organizations mitigate risks but also build trust with customers and partners. Businesses can confidently adopt AI and ML technologies, knowing that their cloud environments adhere to industry standards and regulations.

Looking ahead, the future of AI and machine learning in the cloud within China is promising. As technology continues to evolve, we can expect further advancements in AI algorithms and cloud infrastructure, leading to even more sophisticated applications. Organizations that embrace these developments will likely gain a competitive edge, harnessing AI-driven insights to inform strategic decisions and enhance customer experiences. By investing in cloud-based AI and ML solutions, businesses can position themselves at the forefront of innovation, ready to navigate the complexities of an increasingly digital landscape.

Lesson 2
Edge Computing and IoT

Edge computing is revolutionizing the way data is processed, stored, and transmitted, particularly in the context of the Internet of Things (IoT). In China, where urbanization and technological advancement go hand in hand, the integration of edge computing with IoT is becoming increasingly pivotal. By bringing computation and data storage closer to the location where it is needed, edge computing minimizes latency, reduces bandwidth usage, and enhances the overall efficiency of IoT systems. This is especially crucial for applications that require real-time processing, such as smart city initiatives, autonomous vehicles, and industrial automation.

The synergy between edge computing and IoT is evident in various sectors across China. For instance, in smart manufacturing, edge devices can analyze data from machinery in real-time, allowing for predictive maintenance and thus minimizing downtime. This capability is essential in a highly competitive market where operational efficiency can significantly impact a company's bottom line. Moreover, with the rising adoption of 5G technology, edge computing can efficiently support the massive influx of data generated by connected devices, providing the necessary infrastructure to sustain growth in IoT applications.

Security is another critical aspect where edge computing plays a vital role in IoT environments. By processing data locally, sensitive information can be kept within the premises, reducing the risks associated with data breaches during transmission to centralized cloud servers. In a country like China, where data sovereignty and privacy regulations are becoming increasingly stringent, this localized approach to data management aligns well with governmental policies aimed at protecting citizens' data. Edge computing not only enhances security but also ensures compliance with local regulations, making it a strategic advantage for businesses operating in the region.

Furthermore, the economic impact of edge computing and IoT integration cannot be overlooked. Companies that leverage these technologies can create new business models and revenue streams.

For instance, by utilizing real-time analytics from edge devices, businesses can enhance customer experiences, optimize supply chains, and develop innovative services tailored to consumer needs. In the context of China's rapidly expanding digital economy, the ability to harness data effectively through edge computing can be a game-changer for startups and enterprises alike, fostering an environment of innovation and growth.

As organizations in China continue to embark on their digital transformation journeys, the combination of edge computing and IoT will play a crucial role in shaping their strategies. IT and cloud professionals must focus on developing robust architectures that support these technologies while ensuring scalability and security. Business leaders should prioritize investments in edge computing solutions to stay competitive in a landscape characterized by rapid technological advancements. Ultimately, embracing edge computing in conjunction with IoT will not only enhance operational efficiency but also position businesses favorably within the ever-evolving cloud computing ecosystem in China.

Lesson 3
5G and Its Impact on Cloud Computing

5G technology is poised to revolutionize various sectors, and its impact on cloud computing is particularly significant. With its high-speed connectivity, low latency, and increased capacity, 5G enables a more seamless integration of cloud services across diverse applications. This new generation of wireless technology allows businesses to leverage cloud resources more effectively, enhancing real-time data processing and analytics capabilities. For organizations in China, where cloud adoption is rapidly accelerating, 5G presents opportunities to optimize operations, improve customer experiences, and drive innovation.

One of the most notable advantages of 5G is its ability to support massive IoT deployments. As businesses increasingly turn to the Internet of Things to gather data and streamline processes, the combination of 5G and cloud computing becomes essential. High-speed connectivity facilitates the transmission of large volumes of data from IoT devices to cloud platforms, enabling organizations to analyze and act on insights more quickly. This empowers companies to make data-driven decisions in real-time, enhancing operational efficiency and creating value across various sectors, including manufacturing, healthcare, and smart cities.

Moreover, 5G enhances edge computing capabilities, which is critical for cloud computing in scenarios requiring low latency. By processing data closer to where it is generated, edge computing reduces the time it takes to send data to the cloud and receive a response. This is especially important for applications such as autonomous vehicles, augmented reality, and remote healthcare services, where milliseconds can make a difference. The synergy between 5G and edge computing allows organizations to harness the power of cloud resources while ensuring rapid response times, thus opening doors to new business models and services.

In addition to improving operational aspects, 5G is set to transform the way businesses engage with customers. Enhanced connectivity enables organizations to deliver immersive experiences through cloud-based applications, such as virtual reality and high-definition streaming. For companies in China, where digital engagement is increasingly vital, leveraging 5G to enhance cloud services can significantly improve customer satisfaction and loyalty.

Businesses can create personalized experiences based on real-time data, thereby fostering deeper connections with their audiences and gaining a competitive edge in the market.

As the rollout of 5G continues across China, IT and cloud professionals must adapt their strategies to capitalize on these advancements. This includes re-evaluating infrastructure needs, exploring partnerships with telecommunications providers, and investing in skills development to harness the full potential of 5G-enhanced cloud services. By embracing this technology, businesses can not only streamline operations but also drive innovation and elevate their service offerings in an increasingly competitive landscape. The convergence of 5G and cloud computing is not just a technological shift; it represents a fundamental change in how organizations operate and deliver value in the digital age.

Lesson 4
Green Cloud Initiatives

Green Cloud Initiatives are rapidly becoming a vital component of cloud computing strategies in China, as businesses across the country recognize the importance of sustainability in technology. As cloud service providers and enterprises increasingly focus on reducing their carbon footprints, various initiatives have emerged aimed at enhancing energy efficiency and promoting the use of renewable resources. This trend is not only driven by regulatory mandates but also by a growing awareness among consumers and investors of the environmental impact of tech operations.

One of the primary drivers behind Green Cloud Initiatives in China is the government's commitment to achieving peak carbon emissions by 2030 and carbon neutrality by 2060. This ambitious agenda has prompted organizations to adopt more sustainable practices, including optimizing data center operations, utilizing energy-efficient hardware, and integrating renewable energy sources. Businesses are now investing in technologies that allow them to monitor and manage their energy consumption effectively, leading to substantial cost savings and a reduced environmental impact.

In addition to government policies, collaboration among industry stakeholders is fostering innovation in green technology. Cloud service providers are partnering with renewable energy companies to power data centers with solar, wind, and hydroelectric energy. These partnerships not only support the transition to cleaner energy but also enhance the reliability of cloud services by diversifying energy sources. Moreover, many providers are implementing advanced cooling solutions and energy management systems that significantly lower power usage effectiveness (PUE) ratios, contributing further to their sustainability goals.

Another crucial aspect of Green Cloud Initiatives is the adoption of circular economy principles within the cloud computing ecosystem. This involves rethinking the lifecycle of hardware and software, from design and manufacturing to disposal and recycling. By focusing on sustainable design and encouraging the reuse and recycling of electronic equipment, companies can minimize waste and lower the environmental impacts associated with cloud infrastructure.

This shift not only benefits the environment but also presents new business opportunities in the growing market for sustainable technology.

As businesses increasingly prioritize sustainability, the competitive landscape in cloud computing is shifting. Organizations that embrace Green Cloud Initiatives are likely to attract environmentally conscious customers and investors, enhancing their market position. Furthermore, by investing in sustainable practices now, companies can future-proof their operations against evolving regulations and societal expectations regarding environmental responsibility. The commitment to green cloud practices is not merely a trend; it represents a fundamental shift in how cloud computing will evolve in China and globally, ensuring that technology and sustainability go hand in hand.

CHAPTER 7
BEST PRACTICES FOR NAVIGATING CLOUD COMPUTING IN CHINA

Lesson 1
Localizing Your Cloud Strategy

Localizing your cloud strategy is essential for organizations operating in the dynamic landscape of China. The unique regulatory environment, cultural nuances, and market expectations necessitate a tailored approach to cloud computing. IT professionals and business leaders must consider how local laws, data sovereignty requirements, and consumer preferences impact their cloud deployment and management. A one-size-fits-all approach will likely lead to compliance challenges and hinder the ability to connect with local customers effectively.

Understanding the regulatory framework is the first step in localizing your cloud strategy. China's Cybersecurity Law (CSL) and various data protection regulations impose strict requirements on data handling, storage, and transfer. Companies must ensure that their cloud services comply with these laws, which often means partnering with local cloud providers or establishing local data centers. This compliance not only mitigates legal risks but also builds trust with Chinese consumers, who increasingly value data privacy and security.

Cultural considerations play a significant role in shaping cloud strategies. The user experience in China is influenced by local preferences and behaviors, which differ from those in Western markets. IT professionals must tailor cloud applications and services to reflect these preferences, such as integrating popular payment systems (Alipay, WeChat Pay), social media platforms (WeChat, Douyin, Weibo), and user interfaces that resonate with Chinese consumers. Understanding local trends and consumer behavior can enhance user engagement and drive adoption of cloud services.

Collaboration with local partners is another critical aspect of localizing cloud strategies. Establishing relationships with local cloud providers, technology partners, and regulatory bodies can facilitate smoother operations and compliance. These partnerships can provide valuable insights into the local market, help navigate regulatory requirements, and offer access to established networks. For startups and enterprises alike, leveraging local expertise can accelerate growth and innovation in the cloud space.

Finally, continuous evaluation and adaptation of your cloud strategy are vital in the rapidly evolving Chinese market. As regulations change, consumer behaviors shift, and new technologies emerge, organizations must remain agile. Regularly assessing the effectiveness of your localized cloud strategy and making necessary adjustments will ensure that your organization stays competitive. This proactive approach not only enhances operational efficiency but also positions your brand as a responsive and responsible player in the Chinese cloud computing landscape.

Lesson 2
Avoiding Common Pitfalls

In the rapidly evolving landscape of cloud computing in China, IT professionals and business leaders must be vigilant in avoiding common pitfalls that can derail projects and hinder progress. One prevalent issue is the underestimation of regulatory compliance. The Chinese government has implemented stringent data privacy and cybersecurity laws, which can pose significant challenges for organizations. It is crucial for stakeholders to stay informed about the latest regulations, including the Cybersecurity Law and the Personal Information Protection Law. Failing to comply with these regulations not only results in hefty fines but can also damage a company's reputation and hinder its ability to operate effectively in the market.

Another common pitfall is the lack of a clear cloud strategy. Many organizations enter the cloud space without a well-defined plan, leading to fragmented deployments and inefficient resource utilization. IT and cloud professionals should prioritize developing a comprehensive cloud strategy that aligns with business objectives. This strategy should encompass aspects such as workload optimization, cost management, and scalability. A clear roadmap will not only guide the organization in its cloud journey but also facilitate better decision-making and resource allocation throughout the process.

Overlooking vendor lock-in is another significant risk that can affect cloud adoption in China. Many organizations choose cloud providers based on immediate needs without considering long-term implications. Relying heavily on a single vendor can result in challenges related to flexibility and innovation. To mitigate this risk, businesses should adopt a multi-cloud strategy, allowing them to leverage the strengths of different providers and avoid dependence on any one platform. This approach not only enhances resilience but also encourages competition among vendors, ultimately benefiting the organization through better pricing and service options. Additionally, inadequate training and support for staff can lead to operational inefficiencies and increased frustration. Even with the best technology in place, if employees do not possess the necessary skills to utilize cloud services effectively, the organization may not realize the full potential of its investments.

IT leaders should prioritize training and professional development programs that equip staff with the knowledge and skills needed to navigate the complexities of cloud computing. By fostering a culture of continuous learning, organizations can enhance productivity and innovation while ensuring that their workforce is prepared for the challenges of a cloud-centric environment.

Lastly, neglecting to measure and analyze cloud performance can result in missed opportunities for optimization. Many organizations implement cloud solutions but fail to establish key performance indicators (KPIs) to assess their effectiveness. Regular monitoring and analysis of cloud performance can provide valuable insights into resource usage, cost efficiency, and service quality. By leveraging analytics tools, businesses can identify areas for improvement and make data-driven decisions that enhance their cloud strategy. Continuous assessment not only ensures that organizations remain agile and responsive to changing market conditions but also positions them for sustained growth in the competitive landscape of cloud computing in China.

Lesson 3
Building Strategic Partnerships

Building strategic partnerships in the realm of cloud computing is essential for organizations aiming to thrive in China's rapidly evolving market. As businesses increasingly leverage cloud technologies to enhance their operations, the need for collaboration with local and international partners becomes paramount. Such partnerships can provide access to innovative solutions, a deeper understanding of the regulatory landscape, and enhanced market reach. By forging alliances with technology vendors, system integrators, and consulting firms, organizations can accelerate their cloud adoption journey and improve their competitive edge.

One of the key aspects of building strategic partnerships is identifying the right collaborators. IT and cloud professionals must look for partners that complement their strengths and fill in the gaps in their offerings. This includes evaluating the technical capabilities of potential partners, their market presence, and their understanding of local customer needs. In China, where the cloud landscape is characterized by a mix of global and local players, forming alliances with established local providers can offer critical insights into consumer behavior and regulatory compliance. Moreover, these partnerships can facilitate entry into new markets and help navigate the complexities of local business practices.

Trust and communication are foundational elements of successful partnerships. Establishing a strong working relationship requires clear and consistent communication regarding goals, expectations, and responsibilities. IT leaders must invest time in building rapport with their partners, ensuring that both parties are aligned in their vision for the partnership. Regular meetings, joint strategy sessions, and collaborative projects can help foster a culture of trust and open dialogue. Furthermore, leveraging technology such as collaborative tools and cloud-based platforms can enhance communication and streamline workflows, making it easier for teams to work together effectively.

In addition to technical collaboration, strategic partnerships should also focus on co-innovation. The cloud computing landscape is constantly evolving, with new technologies and trends emerging at a rapid pace.

By working together, partners can share their expertise and resources to develop new products and services that meet the demands of the market. For instance, companies can collaborate on research and development initiatives, pilot projects, or joint marketing campaigns to create a competitive advantage. This approach not only benefits the partners involved but also enhances the overall ecosystem, driving innovation across the industry.

Finally, measuring the success of strategic partnerships is crucial for long-term sustainability. Organizations should establish key performance indicators (KPIs) to evaluate the effectiveness of their collaborations. This can include metrics related to revenue growth, market share, customer satisfaction, and operational efficiency. Regularly reviewing these metrics allows businesses to identify areas for improvement and refine their partnership strategies over time. By maintaining a focus on continuous improvement and adaptability, organizations can ensure that their strategic partnerships remain relevant and beneficial in the dynamic landscape of cloud computing in China.

Lesson 4
Future Outlook and Predictions

The future of cloud computing in China is poised for significant transformation, driven by rapid technological advancements and an evolving regulatory landscape. As the Chinese government continues to prioritize digitalization and innovation, the cloud sector is expected to experience accelerated growth. Investment in infrastructure, particularly in data centers and network capabilities, will enhance the reliability and reach of cloud services. Furthermore, the integration of artificial intelligence and machine learning with cloud computing will enable more sophisticated data analytics, fostering improved decision-making processes for businesses.

One of the key trends anticipated in the near future is the rise of hybrid and multi-cloud environments. Organizations in China are increasingly recognizing the benefits of utilizing multiple cloud platforms to enhance flexibility, security, and scalability. This shift will encourage cloud service providers to develop more interoperable solutions that allow seamless data transfer and workload management across different cloud environments. As businesses seek to optimize their operations and reduce costs, the demand for hybrid solutions will drive innovation and competition among cloud providers.

Cybersecurity will remain a paramount concern as cloud adoption expands. In response to increasing data breaches and cyber threats, both the government and private sector will prioritize robust security frameworks. Future cloud solutions are likely to incorporate advanced security protocols, including zero-trust architectures and encryption technologies. IT professionals will need to stay abreast of emerging threats and adapt their strategies accordingly to protect sensitive data. Additionally, regulatory compliance will become more complex, requiring organizations to invest in compliance management tools and expertise.

Another notable prediction is the growing influence of edge computing in the cloud landscape. As the Internet of Things (IoT) continues to proliferate, the need for real-time data processing at the edge will drive cloud providers to expand their services beyond centralized data centers. This shift will enable businesses to improve operational efficiency, reduce latency, and enhance user experiences.

Companies across various sectors, including manufacturing, healthcare, and transportation, will leverage edge computing to harness the power of data-driven insights in real-time, fostering innovation and competitiveness.

Lastly, the increasing collaboration between cloud providers and enterprises will shape the future of cloud computing in China. Partnerships will facilitate the development of tailored solutions that address specific industry needs, enabling organizations to harness the full potential of cloud technologies. As startups and established enterprises work together, innovation will flourish, leading to the emergence of new business models and services. This collaborative approach will not only enhance the cloud ecosystem but also contribute to the overall growth of China's digital economy, positioning the nation as a global leader in cloud computing.

CHAPTER 8
RESOURCES AND REFERENCES

Lesson 1
Cloud Service Providers in China

Resource	Link
Alibaba Cloud	https://www.alibabacloud.com
Huawei Cloud	https://www.huaweicloud.com
Tencent Cloud	https://intl.cloud.tencent.com
Microsoft Azure China (21Vianet)	https://www.azure.cn
AWS China (Sinnet & NWCD)	https://www.amazonaws.cn
Baidu Cloud	https://intl.cloud.baidu.com
Kingsoft Cloud	https://en.ksyun.com

Lesson 2
Regulatory and Compliance Websites

Regulatory	Website
Ministry of Industry and Information Technology (MIIT)	https://www.miit.gov.cn
ICP License Application Portal	https://beian.miit.gov.cn
MLPS 2.0 (Multi-Level Protection Scheme)	https://www.cac.gov.cn
Cross-Border Data Transfer Regulations (CAC)	https://www.cac.gov.cn
Personal Information Protection Law (PIPL)	https://www.cac.gov.cn
Cybersecurity Law (CSL)	https://www.mps.gov.cn
Data Security Law (DSL)	https://www.mps.gov.cn

CHAPTER 9
GLOSSARY OF KEY TERMS AND CONCEPTS

Terms	Description
Cloud Region	A cloud region that is physically and logically separated from the provider's global network. In China, foreign cloud providers operate through independent local partners, meaning that Azure China and AWS China are entirely separate from their global counterparts.
Availability Zone (AZ)	A physically separate data center within a cloud provider's region. In China, most cloud providers (Alibaba Cloud, Huawei Cloud, Tencent Cloud) have multiple AZs per region to ensure high availability and disaster recovery.
China's Cybersecurity Law (CSL)	The primary legal framework governing cloud computing and data security in China, requiring data localization, security audits, and government oversight for foreign and domestic cloud operations.
Cloud Service Provider (CSP)	A company that provides cloud computing services, such as Alibaba Cloud, Huawei Cloud, and Microsoft Azure China. In China, CSPs must comply with strict regulatory requirements, including ICP licensing and MLPS 2.0 security audits.
Cross-Border Data Transfer	A highly regulated process in China, requiring businesses to obtain government approval before transferring data outside of China's borders, as per the Data Security Law and Personal Information Protection Law (PIPL).
Data Residency	The legal requirement for companies operating in China to store and process Chinese user data within Chinese borders, enforced by the Cybersecurity Law and Data Security Law.
Great Firewall of China (GFW)	China's internet censorship and monitoring system, which restricts access to foreign websites and services while regulating cross-border internet traffic.

Hybrid Cloud	A cloud deployment strategy combining on-premises infrastructure with public cloud services, commonly used in China due to data localization laws.
ICP License (Internet Content Provider License)	A mandatory government license required for hosting websites or digital services in China. Businesses must obtain an ICP Filing for non-commercial sites or an ICP Commercial License for e-commerce and paid services.
MLPS 2.0 (Multi-Level Protection Scheme)	A government-mandated cybersecurity framework requiring companies to classify and secure their cloud infrastructure based on risk levels, especially critical for finance, healthcare, and foreign enterprises.
Personal Information Protection Law (PIPL)	China's strict data privacy law, similar to GDPR, imposing limitations on personal data collection, storage, and cross-border transfers.
Reserved Instances	A cost-saving cloud pricing model where businesses commit to a long-term (1-3 year) contract in exchange for discounted cloud service rates.
Security Compliance Certification	Mandatory security audits and certifications for businesses operating in China's cloud market, ensuring compliance with MLPS 2.0, CSL, and industry-specific regulations.
Sinnet	The Chinese company that operates AWS China (Beijing region) under government regulations restricting foreign cloud ownership.
21Vianet	The Chinese company that operates Microsoft Azure China under government regulations restricting foreign cloud ownership.

VPN (Virtual Private Network)	A service that enables secure internet connections and encrypted data transmission. In China, VPN usage is heavily regulated, and only state-approved VPNs are legal for business use.

www.ingramcontent.com/pod-product-compliance
Lightning Source LLC
LaVergne TN
LVHW051536050326
832903LV00033B/4269

* 9 7 9 8 3 1 0 2 6 2 8 6 7 *